TRUMP TWEETS

*A Collection of Donald Trump's Most
Outrageous, Offensive, and Deleted
Tweets From Trump's Twitter Page*

TONY ROBSON

Table of Contents

Introduction

Thank you for downloading Trump Tweets: A Collection of Donald Trump's Most Outrageous, Offensive, and Deleted Tweets From Trump's Twitter Page.

Within this book you will laugh, be outraged, and possibly cry at all of the outrageous tweets that Donald Trump has sent since he joined the Twitter-sphere. The tweets you are about to read span several years, from when he was simply a political pundit, all the way to winning the presidency.

Please note that this is intended to be a fun, lighthearted book, and is not intended to portray any political biases of any kind. It is also not meant to glorify what Mr. Trump has said, but simply to call attention that he did in fact say it on the Internet.

Without further ado, I hope you enjoy these shocking, entertaining, and amazing tweets from Donald Trump.

Offensive Tweets

Donald J. Trump ✔
@realDonaldTrump

Barney Frank looked disgusting--nipples protruding--in his blue shirt before Congress. Very very disrespectful.

1:36 AM · Dec 22, 2011

14,075 RETWEETS   **15,972** LIKES

The first offensive tweet targets US Politician and Signature Bank owner Barney Frank. Barney is known to be a rival of Trump's, but Trump's targeting of his rival seems a bit embarrassing. Instead of commenting on the content of a speech Barney was giving, he instead decided to target Frank's outfit, and his broad stature wearing the outfit. Calling it "disrespectful".

Donald J. Trump ✓
@realDonaldTrump

.@ariannahuff is unattractive both inside and out. I fully understand why her former husband left her for a man- he made a good decision.

7:54 PM · Aug 28, 2012

7,548 RETWEETS   **6,291** LIKES

This tweet is directed towards The Huffington Post's Chief Editor Arianna Huffington. Reacting to an article and the news outlet's stance on not endorsing Trump, Trump comments on Arianna's personal life and her past relationships. A bit ruthless to say the least.

Donald J. Trump ✓
@realDonaldTrump

The Oscars were a great night for Mexico & why not—they are ripping off the US more than almost any other nation.

7:53 PM · Feb 24, 2015

1,183 RETWEETS   **637** LIKES

Even at Hollywood's most prestigious night, Trump doesn't miss the opportunity to create controversy and re-ignite his feud with Mexico.

Donald J. Trump ✓
@realDonaldTrump

Dwyane Wade's cousin was just shot and killed walking her baby in Chicago. Just what I have been saying. African-Americans will VOTE TRUMP!

9:26 PM · Aug 27, 2016

9,329 RETWEETS   **27,747** LIKES

This controversial tweet was made during a sad time for the Wade family and Chicago. I think he should have gone with a little less 'I told you so' and a little more 'I'm sorry for your loss'.

Donald J. Trump ✔
@realDonaldTrump

Our great African American President hasn't exactly had a positive impact on the thugs who are so happily and openly destroying Baltimore!

9:38 AM · Apr 28, 2015

6,790 RETWEETS   **6,477** LIKES

This tweet was sent by Trump during the Baltimore riots in 2015 the death Freddie Gray, a 25-year-old African American man. It blatantly attacked President Barack Obama for the unfortunate situation.

Donald J. Trump ✔
@realDonaldTrump

"@laurasgoldman: .@realDonaldTrump why is it necessary to
comment on .@ariannahuff looks? Because she is a dog who
wrongfully comments on me

8:22 AM · Apr 7, 2015

106 RETWEETS   **159** LIKES

*Back to Arianna Huffington again, and
this time he calls her a "dog" just because
he didn't like comments that were made
on Huffington Post.*

Donald J. Trump ✔
@realDonaldTrump

Isn't it interesting that the tragedy in Paris took place in one of the toughest gun control countries in the world?

3:29 AM · Jan 8, 2015

5,229 RETWEETS　　**5,019** LIKES

Trump again uses a sensitive issue to promote his campaign policies and interests. I'm beginning to notice a trend here.

Donald J. Trump @
@realDonaldTrump

It's Thursday. @billmaher is still a very dumb guy--just look at his past.

1:28 AM · Nov 1, 2013

92 RETWEETS   **86** LIKES

Bill Maher is a TV show host who is often a sharp critic of Donald Trump. It's apparent that Mr. Trump does not take insults to himself very kindly, and often posts his attacks on Twitter.

Funny Tweets

Donald J. Trump ✓
@realDonaldTrump

Man shot inside Paris police station. Just announced that terror threat is at highest level. Germany is a total mess-big crime. GET SMART!

6:24 PM · Jan 7, 2016

12,589 RETWEETS   **15,027** LIKES

In this Tweet, Mr. Trump uses civil unrest in Europe to offer vague advice for them to 'GET SMART!'

Donald J. Trump ✔
@realDonaldTrump

I like Russell Brand, but Katy Perry made a big mistake when she married him. Let's see if I'm right---I hope not.

1:44 AM · Dec 30, 2011

1,009 RETWEETS   **756** LIKES

It's funny that he is later proved correct when Brand and Perry got divorced. Maybe Mr. Trump should work for TMZ?

Donald J. Trump ✓
@realDonaldTrump

.@katyperry must have been drunk when she married Russell Brand @rustyrockets – but he did send me a really nice letter of apology!

2:00 AM · Oct 17, 2014

611 RETWEETS   **561** LIKES

Following the highly publicized divorce, his earlier prediction was spot on! He got his opportunity to boast about something he got right against Russell Brand, who has said some mean things about Mr. Trump in the past.

Donald J. Trump ✔
@realDonaldTrump

An 'extremely credible source' has called my office and told me that @BarackObama's birth certificate is a fraud.

1:23 AM · Aug 7, 2012

15,184 RETWEETS　　**10,850** LIKES

Even though this rumor was high exaggerated, this assurance by Trump is what kick started his Presidential campaign.

Donald J. Trump ✔
@realDonaldTrump

The problem w/ the concept of "global warming" is that the U.S. is spending a fortune on "fixing it" while China & others do nothing!

6:54 PM · Dec 5, 2013

211 RETWEETS   **178** LIKES

China, China, China. When will they ever learn?

Donald J. Trump ✓
@realDonaldTrump

When I said that Hillary Clinton got schlonged by Obama, it meant got beaten badly. The media knows this. Often used word in politics!

8:37 AM · Dec 23, 2015

10,141 RETWEETS   **17,681** LIKES

Personally, I've never heard the term 'schlonged' be used in politics. Any political science experts want to shed some light?

Donald J. Trump ✔
@realDonaldTrump

The cast and producers of Hamilton, which I hear is highly overrated, should immediately apologize to Mike Pence for their terrible behavior

4:22 PM · Nov 20, 2016

26,055 RETWEETS   **105,981** LIKES

While asking for an apology from the cast of Hamilton for his Vice President nominee Mike Pence, he seems to degrade Hamilton. Vice President Mike Pence ignored this gesture and didn't want an apology, and Hamilton is one of the most critically acclaimed plays of our generation.

Donald J. Trump ✔
@realDonaldTrump

How long did it take your staff of 823 people to think that up--
and where are your 33,000 emails that you deleted?

> **Hillary Clinton** @HillaryClinton
> Delete your account. twitter.com/realDonaldTrum...

1:40 AM · Jun 10, 2016

168,493 RETWEETS   **296,889** LIKES

While people may have liked Hillary's modern and youthful reply to Trump with "Delete your Account", Trump's response is funnier in how he actually uses a legitimate issue of her emails to respond back to her.

Donald J. Trump ✅
@realDonaldTrump

Sorry losers and haters, but my I.Q. is one of the highest -and you all know it! Please don't feel so stupid or insecure,it's not your fault

6:37 AM · May 9, 2013

61,079 RETWEETS   **55,477** LIKES

Maybe using proper grammar would flaunt your intelligence in a better way, Mr. Trump.

Donald J. Trump ✓
@realDonaldTrump

For all of the haters and losers out there sorry, I never went Bankrupt -- but I did build a world class company and employ many people!

4:21 PM · Apr 18, 2015

435 RETWEETS   **716** LIKES

Funny thing about this tweet is, it was later proven that Trump's businesses had gone bankrupt 4-5 times.

Donald J. Trump ✓
@realDonaldTrump

I'm at Trump Int'l Hotel in Las Vegas, tallest/most beautiful building in town. Speaking to another great crowd at Treasure Island (12 noon)

9:12 PM · Oct 8, 2015

1,995 RETWEETS   **2,980** LIKES

This tweet basically encompasses Trump perfectly. I, for one, am reading this tweet in Donald's incredible and amazing voice.

Donald J. Trump ✅
@realDonaldTrump

Lightweight Marco Rubio was working hard last night. The problem is, he is a choker, and once a choker, always a choker! Mr. Meltdown.

9:38 PM · Feb 26, 2016

4,860 RETWEETS   **14,228** LIKES

Trump had come up with a lot of sarcastic nicknames of his fellow candidates that defined their behavior and past performances. In this, he targets Republican Marco Rubio, in which he once stalled in a speech, stuttered, with Trump pouncing on the opportunity and calling him Lightweight Marco Rubio, a choker.

Donald J. Trump ✔
@realDonaldTrump

I refuse to call Megyn Kelly a bimbo, because that would not be politically correct. Instead I will only call her a lightweight reporter!

4:44 PM · Jan 27, 2016

7,199 RETWEETS   **19,991** LIKES

Passive aggressiveness at it's finest.

Donald J. Trump ✅
@realDonaldTrump

So far the Super Bowl is very boring - not nearly as exciting as politics - MAKE AMERICA GREAT AGAIN!

7:03 AM · Feb 8, 2016

15,706 RETWEETS   **30,566** LIKES

One thing's for sure, Trump knows how to capitalize when social media sites are trending.

Donald J. Trump ✔
@realDonaldTrump

Everyone knows I am right that Robert Pattinson should dump Kristen Stewart. In a couple of years, he will thank me. Be smart, Robert.

1:48 AM · Oct 23, 2012

50,291 RETWEETS   **55,009** LIKES

Relationship expert Donald Trump strikes again!

Donald J. Trump ✔
@realDonaldTrump

Hillary Clinton should not be given national security briefings in that she is a lose cannon with extraordinarily bad judgement & insticts.

5:57 AM · Jul 30, 2016 from Denver, CO

11,972 RETWEETS   **38,743** LIKES

Trump has never been described as a loose cannon ever, in his entire life. Ever.

Terrifying Tweets

Donald J. Trump ✔
@realDonaldTrump

In addition to winning the Electoral College in a landslide, I won the popular vote if you deduct the millions of people who voted illegally

1:30 AM · Nov 28, 2016

53,197 RETWEETS   **158,296** LIKES

"Rigged! It's all rigged! Even when I win!"

Donald J. Trump ✓
@realDonaldTrump

Lyin' Ted Cruz just used a picture of Melania from a G.Q. shoot in his ad. Be careful, Lyin' Ted, or I will spill the beans on your wife!

6:53 AM · Mar 23, 2016

16,508 RETWEETS   **36,617** LIKES

When calling a fellow candidate a liar isn't bad enough, make sure to make threats for using a public photo!

Donald J. Trump ✓
@realDonaldTrump

If Cuba is unwilling to make a better deal for the Cuban people, the Cuban/American people and the U.S. as a whole, I will terminate deal.

7:02 PM · Nov 28, 2016

23,651 RETWEETS   **79,249** LIKES

Everyone wants there to be a compromise for the betterment of the people, but to threaten to terminate the deal as a whole if Trump's own terms aren't fulfilled might cause dangerous consequences for people in both countries.

Donald J. Trump ✔
@realDonaldTrump

The concept of global warming was created by and for the
Chinese in order to make U.S. manufacturing non-competitive.

12:15 AM · Nov 7, 2012

104,631 RETWEETS   **66,191** LIKES

*A harsh assessment by Mr. Trump
towards global warming and China.*

Donald J. Trump ✔
@realDonaldTrump

Appreciate the congrats for being right on radical Islamic terrorism, I don't want congrats, I want toughness & vigilance. We must be smart!

9:43 PM · Jun 12, 2016

27,106 RETWEETS   **73,290** LIKES

Mr. Trump reminds me of Batman, in the way he talks of 'toughness & vigilance'. Which reminds me, Mr. Trump, what were you doing between the hours of 10pm and 6am last night?

Donald J. Trump ✔
@realDonaldTrump

Healthy young child goes to doctor, gets pumped with massive shot of many vaccines, doesn't feel good and changes - AUTISM. Many such cases!

5:35 PM · Mar 28, 2014

9,509 RETWEETS   **6,954** LIKES

Autism... Not even once!

Donald J. Trump ✔
@realDonaldTrump

Did Crooked Hillary help disgusting (check out sex tape and past)
Alicia M become a U.S. citizen so she could use her in the debate?

2:30 PM · Sep 30, 2016

18,081 RETWEETS   **36,170** LIKES

Where can I find this sex tape? For
research purposes, of course.

Donald J. Trump ✔
@realDonaldTrump

It's freezing and snowing in New York--we need global warming!

12:24 AM · Nov 8, 2012

3,472 RETWEETS   **1,859** LIKES

Maybe you can organize a protest for that, Mr. Trump.

Donald J. Trump ✔
@realDonaldTrump

I'm not against vaccinations for your children, I'm against them in 1 massive dose.Spread them out over a period of time & autism will drop!

8:10 PM · Sep 4, 2014

606 RETWEETS   **728** LIKES

Mr. Trump is obviously unafraid of the touchiest of subjects. Sometimes I wish we could see some statistics from his Tweets.

Donald J. Trump ✓
@realDonaldTrump

Refugees from Syria are now pouring into our great country. Who knows who they are - some could be ISIS. Is our president insane?

6:54 PM · Nov 17, 2015

16,265 RETWEETS   **27,472** LIKES

Didn't Mr. Trump watch the 60 Minutes story about the Syrian Refugees and the extremely long and thorough vetting process they have to go through?

Donald J. Trump ✔
@realDonaldTrump

If the people so violently shot down in Paris had guns, at least they would have had a fighting chance.

3:28 AM · Jan 8, 2015

1,984 RETWEETS   **1,251** LIKES

Little known fact - a time of mourning is the best opportunity to push a political agenda.

Donald J. Trump ✔
@realDonaldTrump

This very expensive GLOBAL WARMING bullshit has got to stop. Our planet is freezing, record low temps,and our GW scientists are stuck in ice

5:39 AM · Jan 2, 2014

6,781 RETWEETS **4,402** LIKES

Mr. Trump knows all. Even more than scientists who do this for a living.

Deleted Tweets

Donald J. Trump (R) @realDonaldTrump

Saturday's attacks show that failed Obama/Hillary Clinton polices won't keep us safe! I will Make America Safe Again!

Deleted after 10 hours at 9:18 AM on 19 Sep, via Twitter for iPhone.

reply

retweet

In the wake of mass shootings in Chicago, Trump took this opportunity to showcase his insensitivity and promotional prowess in such a sensitive moment. No wonder he deleted the tweet.

Donald J. Trump (R) @realDonaldTrump

If dopey Mark Cuban of failed Benefactor fame wants to sit in the front row, perhaps I will put Jennifer Flowers right alongside of him!

Deleted after 43 minutes at 1:23 PM on 24 Sep, via Twitter for Android.

reply

retweet

Touching on another scandalous subject and also defaming Dallas Mavericks owner Mark Cuban, he threatens to have Former President Bill Clinton's supposed mistress Jennifer Flowers sit alongside him in the debate.

Donald J. Trump (R) @realDonaldTrump

Clinton made a false ad about me where I was imitating a reporter GROVELING after he changed his story. I would NEVER Moch disabled. Shame!

Deleted after 22 minutes at 4:20 PM on 12 Jun, via Twitter for Android.

reply

retweet

Referring to a Clinton ad as well as his own disgusting antics of mocking a disabled reporter, he tweets to debunk the FACT but later deleted the tweet because he found out it actually did happen.

Donald J. Trump (R) @realDonaldTrump

These politicians like Cruz and Graham, who have watched ISIS and many other problems develope for years, do nothing to make thing better!

Deleted after 5 minutes at 10:18 AM on 24 Mar, via Twitter for Android.

reply

retweet

Attacking his own party after some were rumored to be against his supposed policies, Trump tries to belittle the competence of Lindsey Graham and Ted Cruz, senior Republican officials.

Donald J. Trump (R) @realDonaldTrump

Ted Cruz didn't win Iowa, he illegally stole it. That is why all of the polls were so wrong any why he got more votes than anticipated. Bad!

Deleted after 1 minute at 8:41 AM on 03 Feb, via Twitter for Android.

reply

retweet

Then further in his attack on the party, he specifies Ted Cruz and his win in the state of Iowa, calling it rigged because of his "expected supposition".

Donald J. Trump (R) @realDonaldTrump

Sour Mitt Romney, who ran the worst campaign in presidential history in losing to Obama, is now pushing Kasich. Tell Mitt where to go, vote T

Deleted after 1 hour at 8:13 AM on 15 Mar, via Twitter for Android.

reply

retweet

Targeting former Presidential candidate and Republican Mitt Romney this time, Trump is belittling him due to Romney's endorsement of John Kasich rather than endorsing him.

Donald J. Trump (R) @realDonaldTrump

Can you believe thatTed Cruz, who has been killing our country on trade for so long, just put out a Wisconsin ad talking about trade?

Deleted after 2 minutes at 5:50 PM on 01 Apr, via Twitter Web Client.

reply

retweet

Donald J. Trump (R) @realDonaldTrump

I have millions more votes hundreds more dels than Cruz or Kasich and yet am not being treated properly by the Republican Party or the RNC.

Deleted after 8 minutes at 10:19 AM on 29 Mar, via Twitter for Android.

reply

retweet

With things getting heated between the party officials, Trump goes on a full on attack against the party as he feels he's being disrespected due to his 'popularity'. Blaming Cruz's trade policies on the country's trade performance and him and Kasich's lack of popularity.

Donald J. Trump @realDonaldTrump · 14h

Lying Ted Cruz and lightweight choker Marco Rubio teamed up last night in a last ditch effort to stop our great movement. They failed!

↩ ♺ 4.4K ♥ 13K •••

Marco Rubio alongside Ted Cruz now, Trump blames them for hindering his campaign trail, and demeaning him as a Presidential candidate.

Donald J. Trump ⬦
@realDonaldTrump

I love Amercia, but politicians make me sick. If I ever run for president, then please shoot me. Let's hope these socialists haven't taken our guns by that point.

18027   **32716**
RETWEETS   FAVORITES

8:44 PM - 20 Jan 2008 · via Twitter · Embed this Tweet

← Reply 🗑 Delete ⭐ Favorite

Well, well, well...

Donald J. Trump ✓
@realDonaldTrump

"@mplefty67: If Hillary Clinton can't satisfy her husband what makes her think she can satisfy America?" @realDonaldTrump #2016president"

4/16/15, 5:22 PM

100 RETWEETS **113** FAVORITES

In this Tweet, Trump attacks his Democratic opposition, Hillary Clinton, questioning her integrity and status as a wife.

Sources Used:

- https://twitter.com/realDonaldTrump/status/149589104168939520

- https://twitter.com/realDonaldTrump/status/240462265680289792

- https://twitter.com/realDonaldTrump/status/570235124178161665

- https://twitter.com/realDonaldTrump/status/769571710924263424

- https://twitter.com/realDonaldTrump/status/592910662424223744

- https://twitter.com/realDonaldTrump/status/585281558816370690

- https://twitter.com/realDonaldTrump/status/552955167533174785

- https://twitter.com/realDonaldTrump/status/396010837623574528

- https://twitter.com/realDonaldTrump/status/685089631973601280

- https://twitter.com/realDonaldTrump/status/522854696663265282

⇨ https://twitter.com/realDonaldTrump/ status/232572505238433794

⇨ https://twitter.com/realDonaldTrump/ status/408595321384476673

⇨ https://twitter.com/realDonaldTrump/ status/516382177798680576

⇨ https://twitter.com/realDonaldTrump/ status/679506175239532545

⇨ https://twitter.com/realDonaldTrump/ status/800298286204723200

⇨ https://twitter.com/realDonaldTrump/ status/741007091947556864

⇨ https://twitter.com/realDonaldTrump/ status/332308211321425920

⇨ https://twitter.com/realDonaldTrump/ status/589388289456660480

⇨ https://twitter.com/realDonaldTrump/ status/652154514997252096

⇨ https://twitter.com/realDonaldTrump/ status/703257866820415488

⇨ https://twitter.com/realDonaldTrump/ status/692312112115380224

- ⇨ https://twitter.com/realDonaldTrump/status/696514666843996160
- ⇨ https://twitter.com/realDonaldTrump/status/260482827458592768
- ⇨ https://twitter.com/realDonaldTrump/status/152490093465186306
- ⇨ https://twitter.com/realDonaldTrump/status/759191265988653056
- ⇨ https://twitter.com/realDonaldTrump/status/232572505238433794
- ⇨ https://twitter.com/realDonaldTrump/status/802972944532209664
- ⇨ https://twitter.com/realDonaldTrump/status/712457104515317764
- ⇨ https://twitter.com/realDonaldTrump/status/803237535178772481
- ⇨ https://twitter.com/realDonaldTrump/status/265895292191248385
- ⇨ https://twitter.com/realDonaldTrump/status/742034549232766976
- ⇨ https://twitter.com/realDonaldTrump/status/449525268529815552

- ⇨ https://twitter.com/realDonaldTrump/status/781788223055994880
- ⇨ https://twitter.com/realDonaldTrump/status/266259787405225984
- ⇨ https://twitter.com/realDonaldTrump/status/507546307620528129
- ⇨ https://twitter.com/realDonaldTrump/status/666615398574530560
- ⇨ https://twitter.com/realDonaldTrump/status/552955075715690496
- ⇨ https://twitter.com/realDonaldTrump/status/418542137899491328

Conclusion

Thank you again for downloading and reading *Trump Tweets: A Collection of Donald Trump's Most Outrageous, Offensive, and Deleted Tweets From Trump's Twitter Page.*

I hope this book was able to give you a great summary of the amazing tweets Trump has sent out over the years.

Since politics are so serious in nature, I wrote this book to show that politics can be entertaining sometimes. Thank you, Mr. Trump, for showing all of us that there is a bright side to politics. Even though sometimes your tweets can be baseless and terrifying.

Once again, thanks again for downloading this book, and I hope you enjoyed it!

Feel free to visit my author page to see the full collection of my e-books here: https://www.amazon.com/Tony-Robson/e/B00IGMY1RW

www.ingramcontent.com/pod-product-compliance
Lightning Source LLC
Chambersburg PA
CBHW071330310526
45789CB00017B/2169